HEADstart

GW01418010

measuring & shape

Shirley Clarke & Barry Silsby

Illustrated by Lorna Kent

BROCKHAMPTON PRESS
LONDON

Research has shown that when children and parents work together at home, the child's work at school improves.

The purpose of the *Headstart* books is to provide activities which your child will enjoy doing and which will encourage learning to take place in the home.

You can help your child get the most out of this book by

- *giving help* where necessary (for example, by reading instructions, helping to fill in a table);

- *reading the advice below.* This gives further information and explains the purpose of each activity;

- *talking* to your child about an activity, to encourage him or her to put thoughts into words;

- *encouraging* your child to be a 'scientist' (by asking why and how things happen and trying to think of ways to find out);

- *showing enthusiasm* and interest in your child's involvement in the book. (Confidence grows with adult approval.)

Pages 4–5   Pet shop problems
This activity involves your child in matching relative sizes without measuring, and in the idea of nesting (that objects fit into bigger containers). Help your child to draw a line from the animal to its house if they are worried about this.

Pages 6–7   True or false
The idea of this activity is to develop your child's use of positional language (words such as above, below and beside). Encourage your child to talk generally about the picture, asking where certain creatures are.

Pages 8–9 Natural symmetry

If your child has difficulty in matching the colours, use a hand mirror placed upright along the middle of the creature to create its mirror image so that the colours will be clearly visible. Make sure your child has all the correct colour felt pens or pencils available.

Pages 10–11 Fill it up

Help your child with the idea of 'full'. Because we often say a container is full when it is not completely filled, children can get confused. Show your child that 'full' means right up to the brim or this activity will not work properly. A waterproof apron would be advisable!

Page 12–13 Shape game

This strategy game should be good fun and provide a good focus for discussion about shapes. The shapes have been labelled to encourage children to use the names during the game. Some of the shapes are irregular so that children will see that a pentagon, for instance, can be any five-sided shape.

Pages 14–15 Shape hunt

The National Curriculum requires that children should recognise these 3D shapes as well as the 2D shapes. Look at cylinders, cuboids and other shapes around the house as they are best described and explored at first hand.

Pages 16–17 My toys

If necessary, help your child to make sure the toys all line up at the bottom as children often do not do this when ordering size. You may need to help your child in using a tape measure. It will be a valuable experience even if they find it difficult to read the numbers.

Pages 18–19 Food

You may need to draw the first line or arrow for your child, as they may lack confidence to begin with. Help your child count up the number of likes and dislikes afterwards. This is a mapping diagram which is a way of representing data.

Pages 20–21 Vegetable survey

This activity involves your child in conducting a survey, following on from the previous activity. You may need to help them with writing the names, but try to encourage your child to do the ticks alone. You may also need to help count up the ticks. Encourage your child to feel important, asking what they have found out at the end.

Pages 22–23 What fits?

This activity is about logical sorting. Your child will need to consider two things at once – size and object for instance. It may be wise to encourage your child to draw with a lead pencil first in case, through discussion, they want to rub out if the object is the wrong size.

Pet shop problems

The pet shop has just had a new delivery of animals.
Can you help the owner put them into the right place?

Draw a line from each animal to their home.
Make sure the home is big enough!

True or false

Look carefully at the picture of Noah's ark.

Underline true or false for each statement.

1 The elephant is under the monkey. True / False

2 Noah is inside the ark. True / False

3 The monkey is next to Noah. True / False

4 The bear is beside the giraffe. True / False

5 The whale is above the ark. True / False

6 The lion is behind the cat. True / False

7 The mouse is on the roof. True / False

8 The bird is above the ark. True / False

Make up some true or false statements of your own to ask someone else.

Natural symmetry

Most creatures are symmetrical.
This means they have the same pattern on
each half of their bodies.

Complete these creatures by colouring in
the black and white half exactly the same
as the coloured half.

Fill it up

Ask a parent if you can do this.

Find two different empty waterproof containers in your kitchen. (Try bottles, plastic bowls, boxes, cups or mugs.)

Perhaps you chose two like this.

Fill one container with water.

Do you think it will pour exactly into the second container?

Or will it overflow?

Or will it not fill it?

Try pouring the water in to find out.

Were you right?

Different shapes make it difficult to tell how much liquid containers can hold.

Collect more containers.

See if you can find two different shaped containers which hold the same amount by pouring water from one to another.

Shape game

A game for 2 players

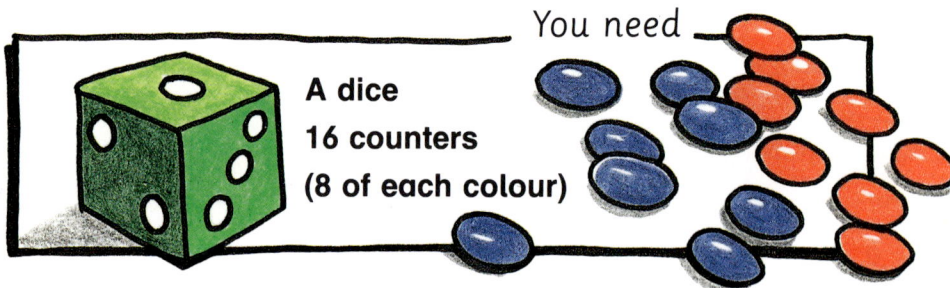

You need

A dice
16 counters
(8 of each colour)

Rules

- Each person rolls the dice.
  The person with the highest score goes first.

- Take it in turns to roll the dice, using a counter to cover a shape with the same number of sides as the number shown on the dice.

- Miss a turn if there are no shapes left with the correct number of sides.

The winner is the first person to get four of their counters in a row up, across or diagonally.

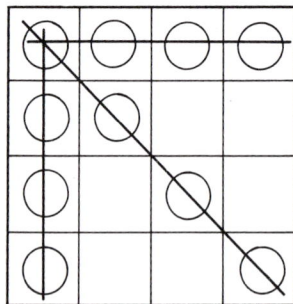

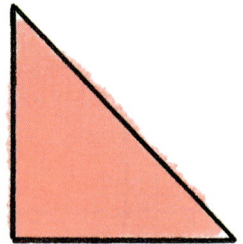

triangle

hexagon

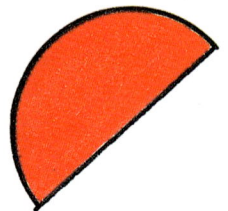

semicircle

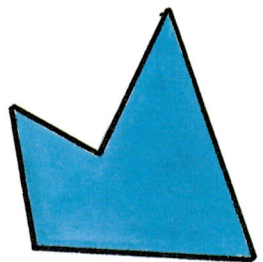

pentagon

oblong	square	circle
circle	semicircle	rectangle
pentagon	triangle	circle
triangle	hexagon	semicircle

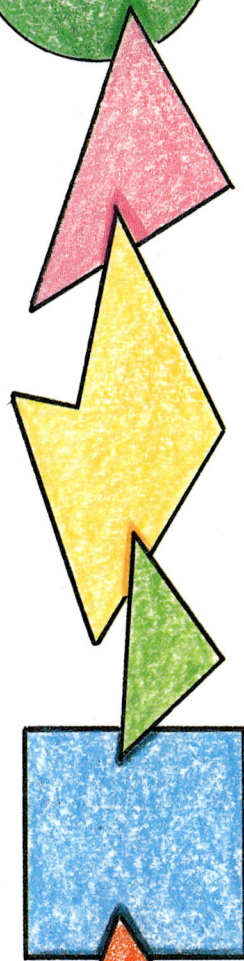

Shape hunt

There are lots of shapes hidden in the toyshop window.

Can you find   3 cubes

   3 cuboids

4 oblongs

   2 triangles

2 spheres

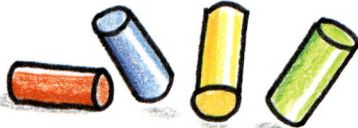   4 cylinders

4 cones

Put a cross on each shape as you find it.

Can you find even more?

14

BOTS
rom
ACE

MADE BY
TOY
MASTERS

Building Blocks

LOTS OF
FUN

DOMINOES

oy Shop

My toys

You need

A tape measure

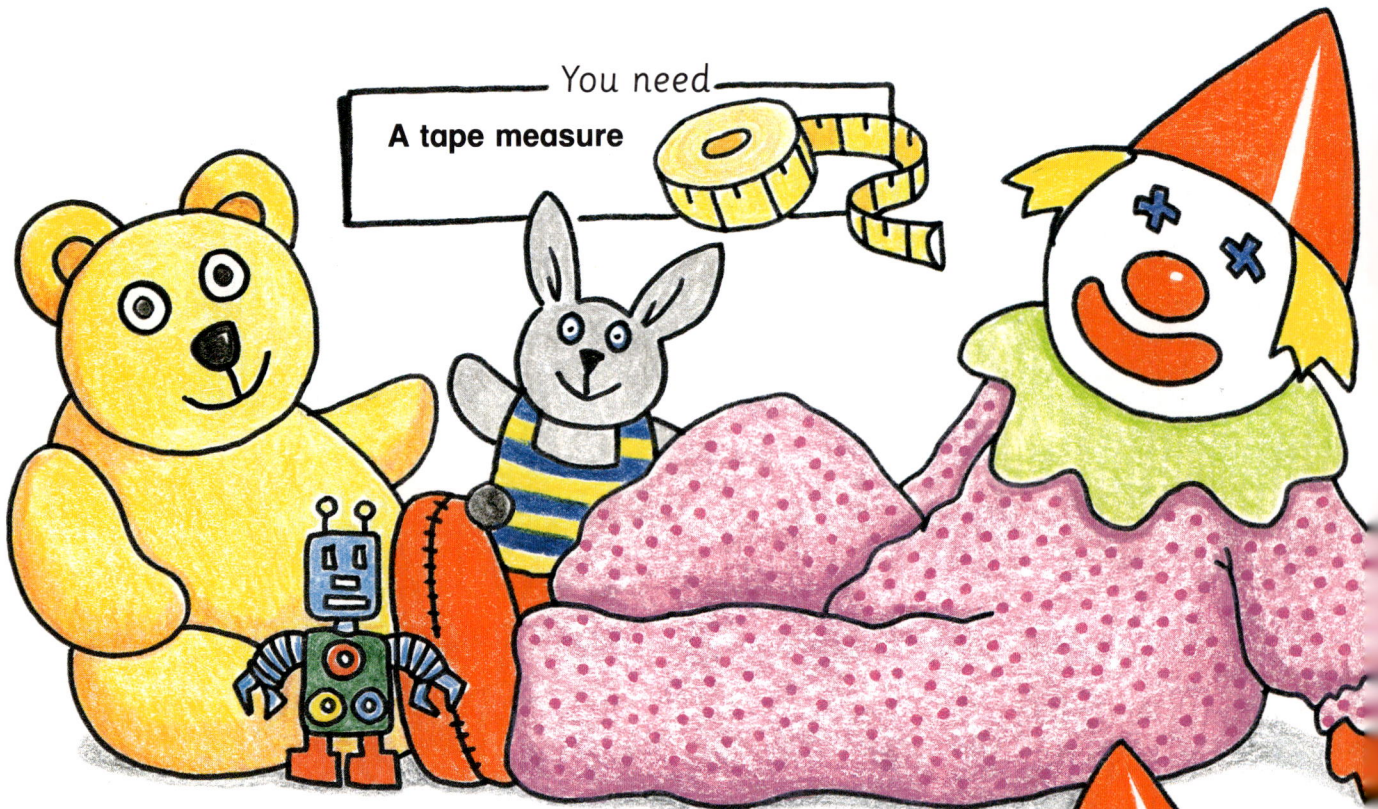

Choose four of your toys to measure.

Lay them out in order of size.

Now use a tape measure to measure their height.
(Ask an adult if you are not sure how to do this.)

Write your toys' names and heights here.

toy's name	height

How tall are you?

my name _____ my height _____

Food

What do you like to eat?

Draw your favourite food on this plate.

Draw your least favourite food on this plate.

18

Do you like these foods?

Draw a line from the foods you like to the ☺

Draw a line from the foods you don't like to the ☹

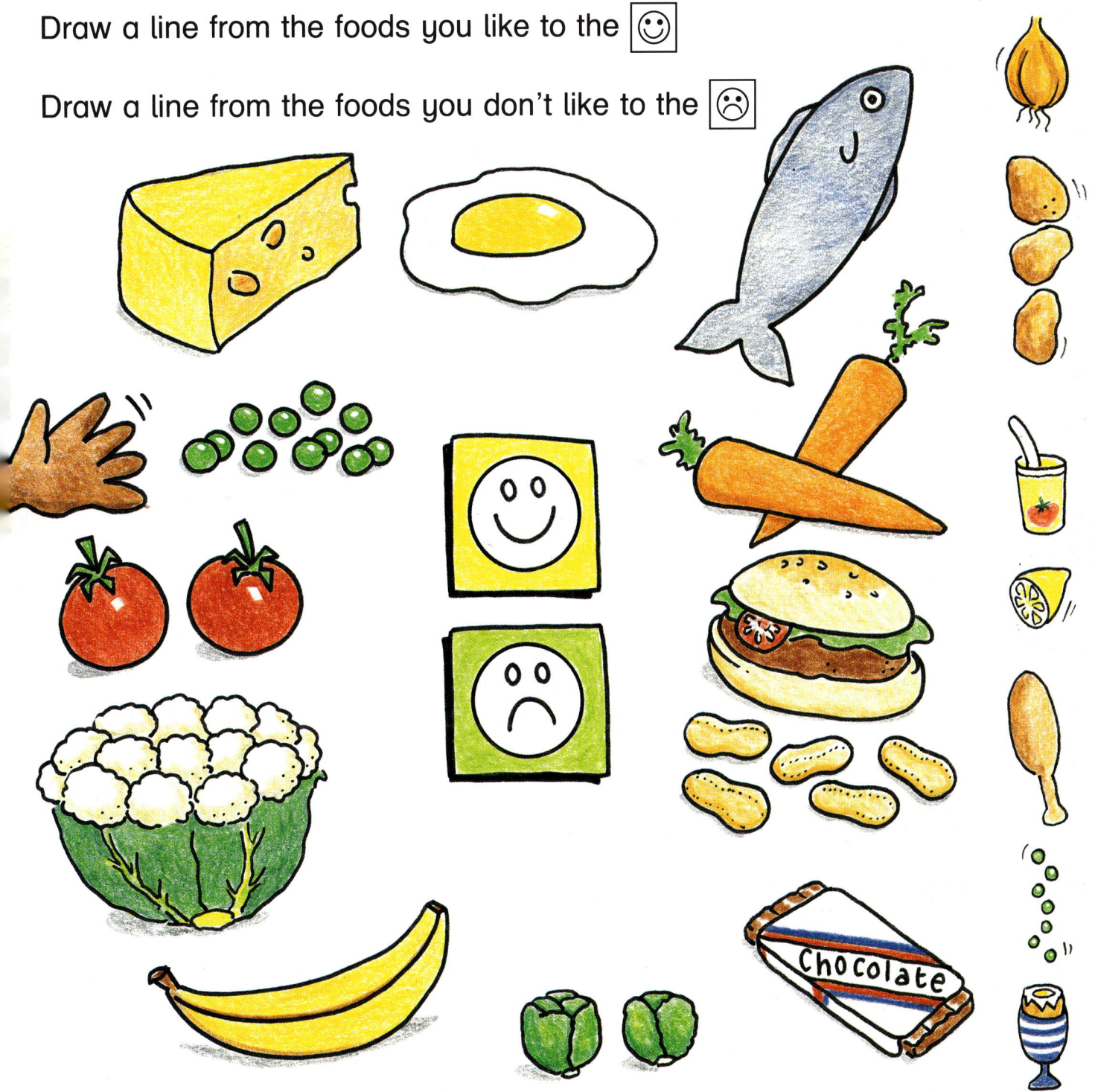

Try this on someone else.

Use a different colour to show which foods they like or dislike.

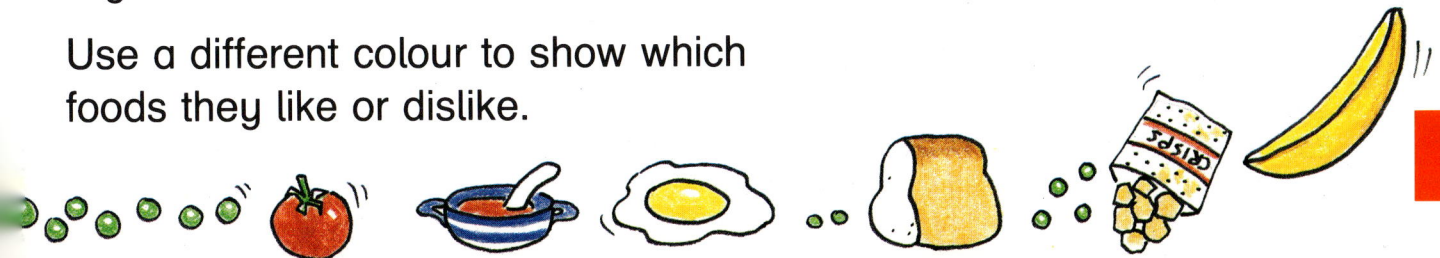

19

Vegetable survey

Find out which vegetables your family likes best.

Fill in your family's names.

Ask them which of these vegetables they like.

Tick all the vegetables they like.

Peas
Sweet corn
Brussel sprouts
Cauliflower

my family's names	peas	sweet-corn	brussel sprouts	cauli-flower	baked beans	cabbage

Count up the ticks and fill in the chart.

vegetable	number of ticks
peas	
sweet corn	
brussel sprouts	
cauliflower	
baked beans	
cabbage	

Which vegetable is your family's favourite?

Make sure you tell the person who cooks the meals what you have found out!

21

What fits?

Look at this:

	red	blue
bus		
car		

The labels at the side tell you what to draw.

The labels at the top tell you how to draw it.

Here is another one:

	tall	short
girl		
boy		

Can you fill in the space?

	big	small
car		
house		

Now fill in one on your own.

green

red

hat

scarf

Can you make up one for yourself?

British Library Cataloguing in Publication Data

Clarke, Shirley
    Headstart: measuring and shape. – (Headstart)
    I. Title   II. Silsby, Barry   III. Series
    372.7

    ISBN 1-86019-521-0
    First published 1991
    This edition published 1997 by Brockhampton
    Press, a member of Hodder Headline PLC
    Group.
    10 9 8 7 6 5 4 3
    1999 1998 1997

Designed and typeset by DP Press Ltd, Sevenoaks, Kent
Printed in India.